CW01652477

Saint Peregrine

Patron Saint of People with Cancer

by
Máire Ní Chearbhaill

All booklets are published thanks to the generous support of the members of the Catholic Truth Society

CATHOLIC TRUTH SOCIETY
PUBLISHERS TO THE HOLY SEE

Contents

Introduction

In the life of the Servite Order for more than 750 years, the sick and the poor have always held a special place. Today, with the apparent increase in cancer, more and more individuals and families ask: "Who is this saint who had cancer? Tell us about him."

His name is Peregrine (pronounced to rhyme with terrapin). He was a Friar Servant of Mary, and his story and relevance are more important today than ever before.

This concise work tells the story of St Peregrine. It is a beautiful story of faith which has given hope and strength to many. The story is told against the historical background of Florence and Tuscany in the thirteenth century, but it points to the same fear and despair felt by many people with cancer in today's world. Finally, in the letters and short glimpses of real-life stories, we are brought into the wonderful area of Christian hope.

This booklet will spread much devotion to St Peregrine and, more importantly, will give new hope and peace where there was only hopelessness before.

In our commitment to service, the figure of Mary at the foot of the cross shall be our model. Since the Son of Man is still being crucified in his brothers and sisters, we, Servants of his Mother, wish to be with her at the foot of those countless crosses in order to bring comfort and redemptive co-operation. (*The Servite Constitutions*)

The Life of St Peregrine

"To so many people, St Peregrine is simply a stranger among the saints. But when the doctor informed me that I had cancer of the lungs, St Peregrine came smilingly into my life.

"I had a problem on earth and was presented with a special advocate in heaven. I was touched with a dreaded disease and blessed with a new and very inspiring friendship."

The words of American writer and broadcaster Fr Daniel Lord, S.J., who died in 1955.

His friend in heaven was Peregrine Laziosi, a thirteenth-century Servite brother, who is known today as the patron saint of people with cancer or malignancy of any kind. This is the story of his life.

Assault on St Philip Benizi

Peregrine was born in the Italian town of Forli in the year 1265. Forli lies about fifty miles north-east of Florence, near the holiday resort of Rimini. At the time of his birth, Pope and Emperor were locked in combat, the one trying to establish his supremacy over the other. Many of the cities and towns in northern Italy became involved in the conflict, some supporting the Pope, others the Emperor; occasionally they switched sides if it suited their cause.

In 1277, when Peregrine was about twelve years old, Forli became the stronghold of anti-papal forces. Pope Martin IV sent an army into the town to re-assert his authority, but there was no surrender. In 1282, he excommunicated the whole town for a period of almost eighteen months. But the conflict dragged on.

Into this deadlocked situation came Fr Philip Benizi, Prior General of the Servite Order. Born in Florence in 1233, he studied philosophy and medicine at the universities of Paris and Padua and went on to join the recently founded Servite Order of friars in Florence. It was mainly through his skills as a diplomat and negotiator that the Order was approved by Pope Benedict XI in 1304.

Philip was visiting the Servite monastery in Forli at the time of the civil conflict, and he agreed to mediate in the dispute. Standing up in the town, he addressed the people and appealed to them to return to obedience to the Pope. But the crowd didn't like what they heard. Shouting and heckling followed. Among the ringleaders of the mob who punched Philip in the face and drove him out of the town was young Peregrine Laziosi.

The townspeople were delighted to be rid of the Servite friar. But Peregrine was less happy with his part in the incident. He had assaulted a priest who had simply acted as a peacemaker. He couldn't rest until he had sought Philip out and asked for his forgiveness.

The Servites

From then on, Peregrine's life changed. The young tearaway became a man of peace and prayer. And he developed an interest in the work and life of Philip Benizi and the friars of the Servite Order.

In the early thirteenth century, with the foundation of the Franciscan and Dominican Orders, there had been a move within the Church to get away from its association with power and material possessions and to return to a simpler way of Christian living.

Against this background, the Order of Friar Servants of St Mary, or Servites as they were called, was founded in Florence in 1233. Originally they were a group of lay people, merchants and traders, who came together to commit themselves to living a simple life of prayer and charitable works, and sharing what they had in a spirit of brotherly love. Some were married, some single. Devotion to Mary played a strong part in their lives, hence the name they were to adopt. Some had been members of the Brothers of Penance, a lay group who ran a hospital in Florence.

At a later stage in their development, a need was felt to deepen their life of prayer. So some of them went up into the hills of Monte Senario outside Florence to live in the caves there and to worship God in solitude. Servite friars still inhabit Monte Senario, living not in the caves but in a fine monastery that looks out for miles over the valley below, with the outline of the city of Florence in the distance.

The original group later came to be known as the Seven Holy Founders of the Servite Order, and were canonised in 1888.

The lay brother

Peregrine was about thirty years old when he entered the Servites as a lay brother. His delay in entry may have been due to difficulties the new Order had in obtaining official recognition. He went to the monastery at Siena to spend his novitiate year. Then he returned to his native Forli, where he remained for the rest of his life.

His days were spent in prayer, in the manual work associated with the running of the monastery, and in visiting the poor and sick in the town.

Right from its beginnings, the Servite friars had become involved in the care of the sick, and some of the Order's oldest records confirm their association with the running of medieval hospitals. St Philip Benizi himself was a medical doctor, but it was Peregrine, a lay brother with no professional training, who was to become known and venerated as the patron saint of those suffering from malignant diseases.

The tradition among religious orders of caring for the sick went back to the early monasteries. Because the monks were often the only people who could read or write, medical books, potions and remedies were entrusted to them. The library at the Benedictine monastery of Monte

Cassino built up a huge collection of ancient medical manuscripts. Ointments and medicines were produced from the herb gardens attached to the monasteries.

In the old abbeys, a monk was appointed specifically to look after the sick of his community in the infirmary, but often he also cared for travellers, pilgrims and local people who fell ill. In this way infirmaries eventually came to be under the care of monks, and it was around monasteries that the early hospitals were built. Moreover, religious orders had the respect of all factions, so in times of war the monastery was often the only place where peace and quiet could be assured for the sick and dying.

Plague in Forli

Brother Peregrine worked tirelessly amongst the sick in Forli and in the surrounding countryside. There were many fatal illnesses and diseases in medieval times which today can be cured. Plagues were one of the great scourges of the time. Towards the end of Peregrine's life the greatest of these, the Black Plague, had appeared in Constantinople. It would make its way via the trade routes to eventually devastate many of the towns and cities of Europe. The stars, storms, and swarms of insects were each blamed for causing the calamity. Overcrowded towns, improper sanitation and poor hygiene would be nearer the truth.

There were several minor epidemics in Italy throughout the first half of the fourteenth century. In 1323 the town of Forli was affected, and Peregrine worked day and night among the dying. The plague was no respecter of persons. Young and old, rich and poor alike fell victim.

Peregrine offered no magic cures or promises of recovery. He simply brought compassion to the dying, and comfort and support for the bereaved. His presence among them as a Servite brother was witness to his faith in a God who continued to care for them and to love them, whatever their sufferings and however long or short their life span on earth might be.

A dramatic recovery

When Peregrine joined the Servite Order, physical penances were very much part of the devotional practices in the monasteries. Hair shirts, fasting, and sleeping on planks were common ways of mortifying the flesh. One of the penances favoured by Peregrine was to stand for long hours in prayer.

It may have been this practice that led in later life to varicose vein trouble. The condition progressively worsened, and one of his legs eventually became ulcerated and malignant. Dr Paul de Salaghis, the local medical practitioner, was called in. After examination, the doctor recommended amputation as the only hope of saving Brother Peregrine's life.

That night, Peregrine lay in bed considering his predicament. Operations in those times, six hundred years before the arrival of anaesthesia as we know it today, could be grim affairs. The practice was to soak a sponge in opium or a similar drug and to apply this to the patient's nose to induce sleep before surgery. Surgical instruments were often crude. Disinfectants were unknown, which meant that many patients died from infection following amputation or other surgery.

So the odds against Peregrine's survival were high, operation or no operation. In the middle of the night and in great pain, he dragged himself out of bed to pray before a crucifix in the monastery chapter room.

An old history of the saint, written in the fifteenth century, records how Peregrine fell asleep in front of the crucifix, and in a dream seemed to see Jesus come down from the cross. He woke up and made his way back to bed.

In the morning the doctor arrived with his instruments to perform the amputation. On examination of the leg he found that the wound had healed and there was no sign of gangrene. The operation was cancelled and the doctor departed in amazement. Word of the dramatic recovery spread like wildfire throughout the town. The Servite brother was restored to health and continued his work among the sick.

Death of Peregrine

Peregrine lived into old age at the monastery in Forli. In 1345 he died, at eighty years of age. His body was laid out in the chapel, and as soon as the news of his death became known, the townspeople crowded into the church to pay their respects. All day long they came, and that night the gates of the town couldn't be closed because people were still arriving in from the surrounding districts. There is a tradition that three people were cured at this coffin: a blind man, a possessed woman, and a man badly injured following a fall.

His own people saw him as someone special in death as well as in life. Peregrine was not buried in the monastery grounds, as was the usual custom; rather his body was placed in the back wall of the Servite Chapel in Forli. There were originally two coffins. The inner coffin was protected by glass and made of gilded wood depicting events in his life. The designs were attributed to a fourteenth-century artist, Baldassare Carrari of Forli. The outer coffin was decorated in a similar manner, probably by Marco Palmezzano (d. 1539). These two coffins have long since disappeared, as the remains were removed and placed in another container during the process of canonisation.

Devotion to St Peregrine

After his death, devotion to Peregrine as an intercessor for the sick began to spread to other Italian cities, especially Venice, Turin and Bologna.

In the early seventeenth century, the case for his canonisation was entrusted to the Jesuit cardinal, Robert Bellarmine, who would later be canonised himself.

Peregrine was beatified in April 1609 with a friend from his novitiate days in Siena, Joachim. Thirty years later, in the midst of a civic reception, his remains were formally placed in a specially built chapel in Forli. Thousands of visitors still call at the chapel every year to visit the remains of the saint contained in a glass case at the back of the altar.

In 1726, Peregrine was declared a saint by Pope Benedict XIII. Canonised at the same time was the great Carmelite mystic, St John of the Cross.

Outside of Italy, veneration of St Peregrine grew, especially in Spain, Hungary and Austria. Another Italian saint, St Veronica Giuliani, developed a great devotion to Peregrine following a cure from an illness.

Peregrine is today the co-patron of the city and diocese of Forli, and in the Amazon region of Brazil a diocese bears his name. His feast is celebrated on 4 May.

St Peregrine and People with Cancer

When the Servites extended their mission to Britain and the United States in the nineteenth century, they brought with them their devotion to St Peregrine as the saint of the sick, particularly of cancer patients. In Ireland, the first Servite house was opened in 1947, and from its beginning Benburb Priory in County Tyrone has been a place where the sick and their families like to come to pray, to find strength in their sufferings or to attend Mass in honour of St Peregrine.

At the St Peregrine Centres, Servites and lay associates run a counselling service for those who have cancer and for their families. Like Peregrine, who worked among the afflicted people of Forli over six centuries ago, the emphasis is on compassion and sympathy, on giving people the opportunity to express their feelings and anxieties when confronted by the crisis of serious illness.

Cancer is still, to most people, a hopeless word. It spells pain, long illness or death. But modern medical advances have brought great relief to cancer sufferers. With surgery, drugs and other forms of treatment, the disease can be cured or controlled in many cases. Expert medical and nursing care helps even the seriously ill to stay relatively comfortable and free of pain.

Yet medical science alone cannot banish the many human problems associated with the illness. Profound shock inevitably follows the diagnosis of cancer in a patient. Shock and fear, disbelief and bewilderment. Feelings of hopelessness and bitterness, anger with God, affect not only the sick but their families and friends.

The St Peregrine Centres provide a service at both the spiritual and the psychological level for those affected by cancer, through individual counselling, letter-writing, visitation of the sick, and prayer. The sick and their families are helped to come to terms with the reality of the disease, so that fear and anxiety are diminished and are replaced eventually by peace and acceptance.

Peter's story

When cancer strikes a family, a common difficulty found in counselling is the inability of loved ones to communicate honestly with the sick person. Peter was a forty-nine-year-old engineer and father of three children. He was in hospital with cancer of the liver. His wife, Maureen, on the suggestion of a friend, called at the St Peregrine Centre to request prayers for his recovery. It was her first introduction to St Peregrine, yet this simple act of faith was to lead on to a whole new level of communication within the family during Peter's illness.

Maureen admitted that she was very bitter and upset. Why Peter? She had been unable to speak about her feelings to anyone, least of all her husband. At his bedside, apart from general sympathetic enquiries about his health and comfort, the subject was carefully avoided. Their conversations were always kept on general topics. The word cancer was never mentioned.

A visit to Peter in hospital revealed that the loneliness and isolation associated with his illness were his greatest problems. He knew he was dying, yet he wasn't able to discuss the situation with his wife for fear of distressing her. Yet so many personal matters needed to be discussed before it was too late.

The opportunity to talk freely to a third person benefited them both. By bringing their feelings out in the open in this way, it became easier for Peter and Maureen to talk about the illness together, even to use the dreaded word cancer. Evasion gave way to openness and honesty. Family affairs were discussed, any requests Peter had, happy memories of the past shared in the precious weeks that were left. Their newfound devotion to St Peregrine gave a direction to their prayers and the courage to accept God's will for Peter. The whole family were drawn together in a way that might never have seemed possible, enabling Peter to let go in peace when the time came.

The power of prayer

Just as it is difficult to accept the news of having cancer, it can be equally difficult to believe that the disease has been arrested. Uneasiness and anxiety linger, and many patients still need support and reassurance to help them adjust to the good news that their treatment has been successful. St Peregrine himself was cured of a malignant disease and was able to continue his work among the poor and sick. In this spirit, patients are encouraged to accept the gift of restored health and to pray for the ability to feel and express gratitude. One such patient was able to write later:

> 'Thanks to the prayers of so many and my prayer to St Peregrine, after my last treatment, the tumour has disappeared. I will continue to pray in thanksgiving for all who have cancer.'

In their daily prayers, the Servites who work in the area of cancer counselling remember those who suffer. At their monthly Masses in honour of St Peregrine, the sick or their relatives and friends are invited to attend, to pray together and draw support and strength from one another.

This regular coming together in faith and prayer has proved a great source of reassurance for many. In the ups and downs and uncertainty of serious illness, the continuity of prayer has a stabilising influence and supplies the impetus to persevere in the face of the unknown.

Helen, a young mother with two children, attributes her will to recover to her perseverance in prayer. She had undergone many treatment sessions and was tired and depressed. There seemed to be no improvement, yet she continued to trust and pray.

Eventually she did respond to her treatment, and before long was coping again with her family and able to return to her part-time job. Her unbroken faith in the intercession of St Peregrine had provided the necessary lifeline for her when all else seemed hopeless.

Miracles of faith

When a person is faced with a terminal illness, it is natural to implore God for a miracle. St Peregrine himself prayed for a cure, believing that everything was possible with God. Yet in counselling these patients, no false hopes or promises of recovery can be offered. Bodily healing alone is not stressed, but the wider healing that comes from the calm acceptance of God's will, whatever the medical prognosis might be. As Fr Daniel Lord, S.J., the American author and broadcaster, said when he was dying of lung cancer:

> 'I have not received a miracle from St Peregrine, but then I have not asked for a miracle. I have worn his medal over my heart and carried and said his prayer… but the peace, the peace: this is miracle enough.'

The miracles received through the intercession of St Peregrine are not the kind that will ever make newspaper headlines. But the letters of thanksgiving that arrive at the

St Peregrine Centres from cancer patients and their families reveal that these miracles are many and varied.

Miracles of faith and acceptance, of healing in spirit, of unity, love and forgiveness within families, and above all, the gift of the peace of Christ.

In a moving letter after the death of his wife, a man wrote:

"From the day she began her devotion to St Peregrine, asking not for a cure but for courage and acceptance of God's will, she changed from a very frightened woman over a period of time and died a very happy death. Her courage spilled over in the family, and we found the strength to nurse her ourselves – something we never thought we could do. We talked about so much that might never have been said – once we accepted her dying. Even now, the peace and joy she felt helps us. We continue to pray to St Peregrine. He has become our household saint."

Devotions to St Peregrine

Prayer

God our Father, Lord of consolation, your son suffered and died so that we might have life. This day we praise the wonder of your love for us in the example of your servant Peregrine. Through his intercession, help us to open our lives to your healing for us, listen to your word, and do your blessed will. This we ask through our Lord Jesus Christ, your son, who lives and reigns for ever and ever. Amen.

Scripture meditations

O God, you are my God, for you I long,
for you my soul is thirsting.
My body pines for you
like a dry weary land without water.
So I gaze on you in the sanctuary
to see your strength and your glory.

For your love is better than life,
my lips will speak your praise.
So I will bless you all my life,
in your name I lift up my hands.

My soul shall be filled as with a banquet,
my mouth shall praise you with joy.
On my bed I remember you.
On you I muse through the night,
for you have been my help;
in the shadow of your wings I rejoice.
My soul clings to you;
your right hand holds me fast.
(*Psalm 62*)

We are afflicted in every way possible,
but we are not crushed;
full of doubts, we never despair.
We are persecuted but never abandoned;
we are struck down but never destroyed.
Continually we carry about in our bodies
the dying of Jesus,
so that in our bodies
the life of Jesus may also be revealed.
(*2 Corinthians 4:8–10*)

Take my yoke upon you and learn from me, for I am gentle and lowly in heart, and you will find rest for your souls. For my yoke is easy and my burden is light.
(*Matthew 11:29–30*)

> As the Father has loved me, so have I loved you; abide in my love. If you keep my commandments, you will abide in my love, just as I have kept my Father's commandments and abide in his love. These things I have spoken to you, that my joy may be in you, and that your joy may be full. (*John 15:9–11*)

Intercessions

God our Father, you are a God who loves me. I thank you for the many blessings you have given me. In loving trust I place myself before you. Let your healing love fill my life.

Give me the strength to understand my illness. Forgive my failures in carrying the cross. In St Peregrine you gave us an example of patient suffering. Supported then by his prayers, I ask that the suffering I endure may be a source of life both now and for ever. I make this prayer through Christ your Son. *St Peregrine, Pray for me.*

Lord, you have known the pain of suffering. Be with me in my pain, and comfort me in my loneliness. Forgive my impatience and bless my efforts to be generous to all.
St Peregrine, Pray for me.

Holy Spirit, bless me with the gift of understanding. Bring healing to my life and to the lives of my loved ones. Send your gift of forgiveness to me and to those I may have hurt in the past. *St Peregrine, Pray for me.*

O God, in St Peregrine you gave us an outstanding example of faith and patience. We humbly ask you that, by imitating him and by the help of his prayers, we will believe more fully in your healing help, bear the sufferings of this life without wavering, and come with joy to the peace of heaven. We ask this through Christ our Lord. Amen.

Further information

Further information on St Peregrine (novena book, medal, prayers) may be obtained from:

St Peregrine Centre
Servite Oratory, Rathfarnham Shopping Centre
Dublin 14, Eire

St Peregrine Centre
Servite Priory, Benburb, Co. Tyrone,
N. Ireland BT71 7JZ

St Peregrine Centre
Servite Priory, Kingsway East, Dundee,
Scotland DD4 8AA

The CTS Bookshop
25 Ashley Place, Westminster Cathedral Piazza
London SW1P 1LT Tel: 020 7834 1363

GLOSSARY

Beatification: stage in the process of canonisation, declaring a person 'blessed'.

Canonisation: process by which the Church declares someone to be a saint.

Declared a saint: the final act in the canonisation process, that someone has lived a life of holiness and christian virtue, an example for all the faithful.

Dominican: someone who lives by the order of St Dominic, in the religious Order of Preachers, founded by St Dominic.

Excommunicated: to be placed 'out of' (ex) communication with the Church.

Fasting: abstaining from food or other pleasures or recreations, as an act of penitence.

Franciscan: someone who lives by the rule of St Francis, in the religious Order of Franciscans, founded by St Francis.

Hair shirt: uncomfortable garment voluntarily worn as an act of penitence.

Novitiate: initial trial period when setting out on the religious life.

Penances: an act of sorrow, seeking forgiveness and reparation for sins committed.

Servite Order: a religious order of people consecrated to God.